Baby Brother's

Bunny

Written by JaTanna Patterson

Illustrated by Wings of Colors

ISBN: 979-8-218-66451-0

This book is inspired by true events. Some elements have been fictionalized. Any resemblance to actual persons is purely coincidental.

Dedication

My dearest Gaea and Giannis,

Giannis, my sweet baby boy in the stars. Your sparkling eyes held the light of a thousand suns. Though your time here was far too short, your love left a forever mark on my soul. You are never forgotten, always cherished, and forever loved.

Gaea, my beautiful baby girl. You are my strength, my joy, my reason. Your laughter lifts me, your spirit grounds me, and your love keeps me going.

One I hold in my arms,

one I carry in my soul,

both are pieces of me,

both make me whole.

I sat on a shelf in a quiet little room. Soft and still. Waiting.

In a house filled with murmurs and the occasional patter of tiny feet, I sat alone, a plush brown bunny with floppy ears, waiting for a little friend. One day, a baby boy arrived. His mommy and daddy named him Giannis.

That's when she came in.
Gia.
All curls and giggles, dancing
through the room like sunlight.
She called him baby brother.

Warm arms wrapped around me,
and tiny fingers tugged my ears.
I was his.

Music filled the house, along with laughter, lullabies, and the sounds of Gia.
She twirled, sang, and celebrated her baby brother's presence.

FOOTSTEPS

But soon, the sounds changed. Hushed voices replaced laughter. Quiet footsteps filtered through the house. Whispers behind closed doors.

One particular afternoon, the crib was quiet. Bottles left untouched. The rocking chair no longer moved. Baby brother was gone.

"Mommy," I heard Gia say,
"where is baby brother?"
Her voice was small.
The room held its breath.

"He's in a special place," Mommy said. "A place where his body doesn't hurt anymore."

Gia didn't understand,
and neither did I.
How could someone
so small
just disappear?

Gia remembered his soft skin.
The way his eyes sparkled.
She missed him deeply.
I could feel it in her hugs.

"Is he playing there?" She asked.
"Can he hear me?"
"Yes, sweet Gia,
I believe he can."

That night, something changed.
Mommy held me close,
closer than ever before.

She gave me to Gia. "This was baby brother's favorite bunny," she said. "Whenever you miss him, hold this tight."

Gia's arms wrapped around me, warm and safe.
Her tears brushed my fur.

"Goodnight, baby brother,"
she whispered.
"I really miss you."

I stayed with her through the night.
And the next.
And the next.
I was hers now, carrying a piece of
him in every stitch.

One morning, Gia spotted
something outside.
A bunny.
Just like me.
Still. Quiet. Watching.

She ran to Mommy.
"I saw a bunny just like baby brother's bunny!"

Mommy smiled.
"Baby brother's spirit is all around us," she said.
"Whenever you see a bunny, you can think of him."

And Gia did just that!
In the backyard, in clouds, in dreams.
Every bunny became a whisper of love.

Gia still twirled.
She still sang.
But now, she held me close
when her heart felt heavy.

She learned that love doesn't disappear.
It just finds a new way to stay.

Even though baby brother
wasn't in his crib,
Gia found him in memories,
in hugs,
in me.

And every time she held me,
he felt a little closer.

I am just a bunny.
But in Gia's arms,
I am something more.
I am the softness of goodbye,
the warmth of forever,
the keeper of a brother's love.